My Science Library

Melting Matter

by Amy S. Hansen

Science Content Editor:
Kristi Lew

To the
Khan Kids

[signature]

Rourke
Educational Media

rourkeeducationalmedia.com

Science content editor: Kristi Lew

A former high school teacher with a background in biochemistry and more than 10 years of experience in cytogenetic laboratories, Kristi Lew specializes in taking complex scientific information and making it fun and interesting for scientists and non-scientists alike. She is the author of more than 20 science books for children and teachers.

www.rourkeeducationalmedia.com

Photo credits: Cover © Brad Collett, mcherevan, Michael C. Gray, mikeledray, Cover logo frog © Eric Pohl, test tube © Sergey Lazarev; Table Of Contents © Monkey Business Images; Page 5 © zulufoto; Page 6 © Mike Flippo; Page 7 © Vince Clements; Page 8 © Ivan Proskuryakov; Page 9 © Jacom Stephens; Page 10 © Monika Hunácková, Christian Lopetz, Blue Door Publishing; Page 11 © JR Trice; Page 12 © Mike Flippo; Page 13 © Monika Hunácková, Christian Lopetz, Blue Door Publishing; Page 15 © Mario Bonotto; Page 16 © Roman Sigaev; Page 17 © Galyna Andrushko; Page 19 © Evlakhov Valeriy; Page 21 © holbox

Editor: Kelli Hicks

My Science Library series produced for Rourke by Blue Door Publishing, Florida

Library of Congress Cataloging-in-Publication Data

Hansen, Amy.
 Melting matter / Amy S. Hansen.
    p. cm. -- (My science library)
 Includes bibliographical references and index.
 ISBN 978-1-61741-752-8 (Hard cover) (alk. paper)
 ISBN 978-1-61741-954-6 (Soft cover)
 1. Fusion--Juvenile literature. 2. Thawing--Juvenile literature. 3. Melting points--Juvenile literature. I. Title.
 QC303.H36 2011
 536'.42--dc22
                                      2011004764

Rourke Educational Media
Printed in the United States of America,
North Mankato, Minnesota

rourkeeducationalmedia.com

customerservice@rourkeeducationalmedia.com • PO Box 643328 Vero Beach, Florida 32964

Table of Contents

Melted Treats Are Still Matter

Want some ice cream? Don't get it until you're ready to eat because ice cream **melts**.

All of our food is made of matter. Some matter tastes really good.

Ice cream is made of **matter**. Matter is anything that has **mass**, or weight, and takes up space. Matter can be a solid, a liquid, or a gas.

Ice cream is a solid when it is cold.

Matter can also change forms. Ice cream melts when it gets warm. It changes from a solid to a liquid.

Melted ice cream may still feel cool.

Ice cream is made of cream and sugar. But at a more basic level, the ice cream is made of **molecules**.

Molecules are super-small units. You can only see them with a powerful microscope. When the molecules in ice cream are frozen, they do not move very much. A solid holds its shape.

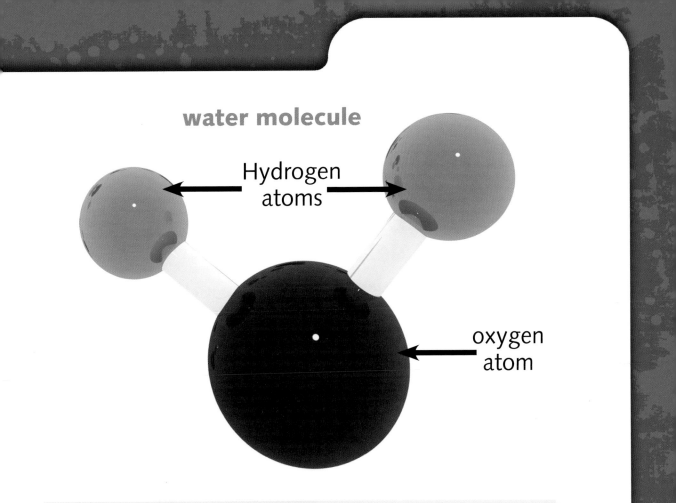

water molecule

Hydrogen atoms

oxygen atom

Atoms are tiny pieces of matter. They combine to form molecules. For example, every water molecule is made of two hydrogen atoms and one oxygen atom.

What Happens When It Melts?

If ice cream gets warmer than 32 degrees Fahrenheit (0 degrees Celsius), it starts melting. That means the molecules move more. They cannot hold a shape. Ice cream becomes a liquid.

A liquid cannot hold its shape. It spreads out.

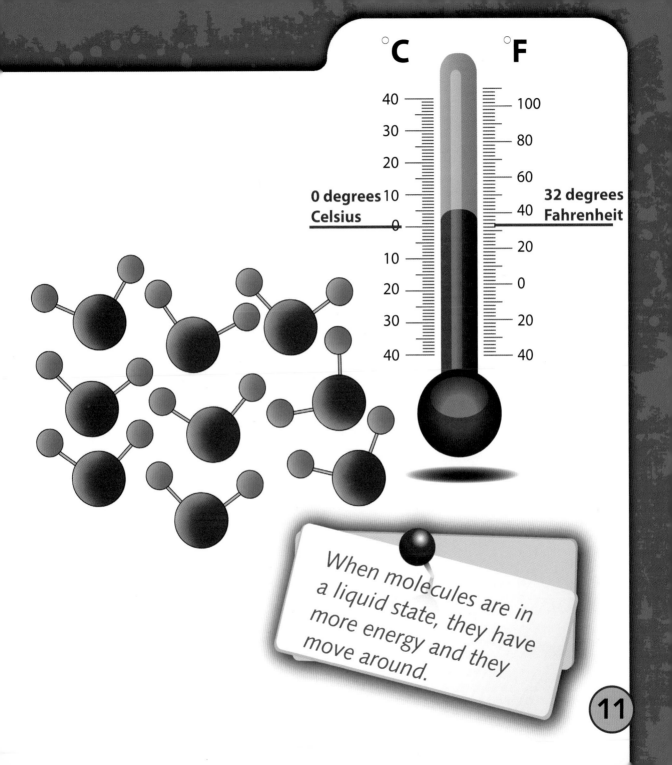

°C

40
30
20
10
0 degrees
Celsius 0
10
20
30
40

°F

100
80
60
40 **32 degrees**
Fahrenheit
20
0
20
40

When molecules are in a liquid state, they have more energy and they move around.

Now **freeze** the melting ice cream. The molecules slow down. Ice cream becomes a solid again.

A solid holds its shape.

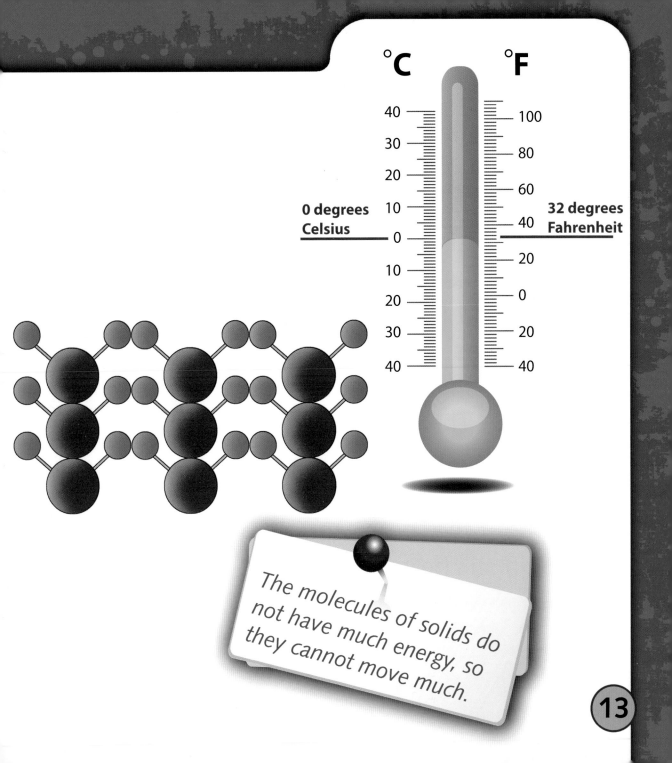

°C   °F

40 — — 100

30 — — 80

20 — — 60

0 degrees   10 — — 40   **32 degrees**
Celsius   0 —   **Fahrenheit**
                  — 20

10 — — 0

20 — — 20

30 — — 40

40 —

The molecules of solids do not have much energy, so they cannot move much.

Is It Melting?

If you stir sugar into water, it looks like it melts into the water. But it doesn't melt, it **dissolves**.

Dissolving is different than melting. The sugar and water molecules move together to make sugar-water. If you could take out the water, the sugar would still be there.

Sugar looks like it disappears in the water, but it is still there.

Not everything melts easily. Look at the glass pan. Glass needs a high **temperature**, at least 1400 degrees Fahrenheit (760 degrees Celsius), before it melts.

Other matter doesn't melt. Wood doesn't melt. It **burns**. We sometimes use it for campfires.

Make a Wish!

Candles melt and burn at the same time. Heat from the flame melts the wax. Then, the flame burns the gas that the melted wax gives off.

Melted wax runs down the candles, but it will be a solid again as soon as it cools.

19

If you want to keep a candle from melting, you don't treat it like ice cream. You don't freeze it. You blow it out.

SHOW What You Know

1. Can you think of something else that melts, besides ice cream or candles?

2. A bar of soap disappears when it is in water. Is it melting or dissolving?

3. Wood doesn't melt, it burns. Can you think of something else that doesn't melt, but burns?

Glossary

burns (BURNZ): set on fire in order to make heat or light

dissolves (di-ZAHLVZ): seems to disappear when combining with a liquid

freeze (FREEZ): to change from a liquid into a solid

mass (MASS): the amount of matter an object has, usually measured in grams or pounds

matter (MAT-ur): something that has mass and takes up space

melts (MELTZ): changes from a solid to a liquid

molecules (MAH-luh-kyools): two or more atoms chemically bonded together

temperature (TEM-pur-uh-chur): the measurement of how hot or cold something is, usually measured with a thermometer

Index

Websites

www.factmonster.com/dk/science/encyclopedia/changing-states.html

www.brainpopjr.com/science/matter/changingstatesofmatter/
   grownups.weml

www.sciencekids.co.nz/gamesactivities/meltingpoints.html

About the Author

Amy S. Hansen is a science writer who lives in the Washington, D.C. area with her husband and two sons. Her whole family loves studying the melting of matter under hot fudge.